MONEY
BLESSINGS

POWERFUL AFFIRMATIONS
FOR ATTRACTING PROSPERITY!

CICELY BLAND

FOREWORD BY NAPOLEON HILL
Think and Grow Rich

Money Blessings: Powerful Affirmations for Attracting Prosperity

Published by Empower House Publishing

New York Information Technology Center

222 Broadway
19th Floor
New York, NY 10038

www.empowerhousepublishing.com
www.moneyblessings.com

Library of Congress Cataloging-in-Publication Data

Bland, Cicely

Money Blessings: Powerful Affirmations for Attracting Prosperity /
by Cicely Bland

ISBN-13: 978-0-9816573-2-5 (trade paperback)

1. Self-help/Prosperity/Inspirational I. Title

Library of Congress Control Number: 2011934826

DEDICATION

In Loving Memory of My Grandparents
William and Ellen Bland
who made valuable deposits into
the vault of my life.

FOREWORD

It is a well known fact that one comes, finally, to BELIEVE whatever one repeats to one's self, whether the statement be true or false. If a man repeats a lie over and over, he will eventually accept the lie as truth. Moreover, he will BELIEVE it to be the truth. Every man is what he is, because of the DOMINATING THOUGHTS which he permits to occupy his mind. Thoughts which a man deliberately places in his own mind, and encourages with sympathy, and with which he mixes any one or more of the emotions, constitute the motivating forces, which direct and control his every movement, act, and deed!

Comes, now, a very significant statement of truth:

THOUGHTS WHICH ARE MIXED WITH ANY OF THE FEELINGS OF EMOTIONS, CONSTITUTE A MAGNETIC FORCE WHICH ATTRACTS, FROM THE VIBRATIONS OF THE ETHER, OTHER SIMILAR, OR RELATED THOUGHTS.

A thought thus "magnetized" with emotion may be compared to a seed which, when planted in fertile soil, germinates, grows, and multiplies itself over and over again, until that which was originally one small seed, becomes countless millions of seeds of the SAME BRAND!

The ether is a great cosmic mass of eternal forces of vibration. It is made up of both destructive vibrations and constructive vibrations. It carries, at all times, vibrations of fear, poverty, disease, failure, misery; and vibrations of prosperity, health, success, and happiness, just as surely as it carries the sound of hundreds of orchestrations of music, and hundreds of human voices, all of which maintain their own individuality, and means of identification, through the medium of radio.

From the great storehouse of the ether, the human mind is constantly attracting vibrations which harmonize with that which DOMINATES the human mind. Any thought, idea, plan, or purpose which one holds in one's mind attracts, from the vibrations of the ether, a host of its relatives, adds these "relatives" to its own force, and grows until it becomes the dominating, MOTIVATING MASTER of the individual in whose mind it has been housed.

~Napoleon Hill
Think and Grow Rich

MESSAGE FROM THE AUTHOR

It is widely known that there is significant mystical power in the number 40 on the account of the frequency of its occurrence in The Holy Bible. In the Bible, 40 (days or nights, years) indicates a cycle of completion and relates to *enlarged dominion, or renewed or extended rule.* Using this ancient wisdom, Money Blessings has been designed for you to achieve immediate and long-term benefits by repeating prosperity affirmations and mentally dwelling on supporting scriptures for 40 consecutive days and 40 nights. Build upon this mindset to completely tap into this miraculous power in order to create more and more of the wealth you desire

Beliefs are simply thoughts that we have been thinking over and over again. Today, I invite you to begin thinking new thoughts about money and your ability to attract it in abundance. Understanding that for many years, you may have been programmed and conditioned to believe in the possibility of lack and limitation, Money Blessings is offering powerful affirmations for you to consistently ponder for 40 consecutive days and nights in order to reprogram and recondition your minds and hearts; thus, developing an entirely new belief system about the infinite possibilities for your ability to attract wealth and prosperity.

For years, I suffered from the appearance of financial lack because of a conditioned belief system that was rooted in thoughts of not having enough money to meet my needs or fulfill my heart's desires. Taking action to abandon past thoughts and create a new belief system changed my life and my financial circumstances for the better. Because of my continued use of the 40 Days of Money Blessings, instead of having stacks of unpaid bills and collection notices, I now have financial plenty to enjoy any way that I choose. Instead of borrowing money to meet my needs, I am able to give abundantly to causes that I am passionate about. Instead of neglecting my health and my family, in order to work more than one job to barely make ends meet, I am able to profit off of what brings me joy and fulfillment.

All of these changes began to happen once I decided to deliberately create more prosperity in my life by the daily practice of using affirmations to develop my prosperity consciousness and release old worn-out beliefs that did not serve my highest good. I now shift my mind away from doubt and skepticism and have a new way of thinking along with improved finances. Today, I share my experiences with you because I want to help you to do likewise.

The key word here is commitment. If you are ready to experience a new life of abundance and prosperity, make a commitment to 40 consecutive days of Money Blessings and observe all the improvements in your finances. If you have been thinking old thoughts of lack and now want to create a bigger fortune for yourself and others, new thoughts are necessary in order to bring about positive changes in your monetary circumstances. If you will read a Money Blessing affirmation and its supporting passage and scripture aloud daily for 40 consecutive days and mentally repeat the daily affirmation throughout the course of the day, especially when confronting appearances of lack, you will begin to attract more money into your life experiences.

In fact, I encourage you to keep a gratitude log or journal throughout the 40 days of Money Blessings and look for at least five things to be grateful for throughout the day. Look for ways that you have been helped financially as you build your prosperity consciousness with the help of the Money Blessings affirmations. Take inventory of inspirations you receive for opportunities to grow your wealth. Write down evidence of financial increase that you experience while practicing the Money Blessings affirmations for 40 consecutive days.

At first some people may find it challenging to commit to 40 days of developing a prosperity consciousness through the use of the Money Blessings affirmations. However, I believe that those who commit to the 40 consecutive days of Money Blessings will have more effective results than those who do not. Yet, that does not mean that someone who commits to Money Blessings for 10, 20 or even 30 days will not begin to see new avenues of financial increase open as well. I have found that the greater the consistent commitment, the better the results. Every moment of every day holds the possibility for financial miracles but we must consistently be expectant and always channel our energies in the direction of that which we desire.

~CICELY BLAND

INTRODUCTION

It's no coincidence that you have opened this book. It means you have made a conscious decision to change your circumstances for the better and live the life you truly deserve. More importantly, your decision to purchase this book and commit 40 consecutive days of your life to unlocking the mysteries of prosperity allows you to utilize your powerful mind to transform your life and your world. Minds are like parachutes – they are only effective when opened. Therefore, by opening your mind now to discovering the hidden relationship between your beliefs and attracting wealth prepares you for unlimited success, fortune and happiness.

Because this book is in your hands, it is evident you have the desire to be free from stress about survival and finances. The key to allowing this freedom begins with opening your mind to your oneness with a greater power. This will not only provide you with the abundance you desire but offer you the peace of mind to enjoy a fuller life filled with unlimited promise.

The purpose of this book is to increase awareness of the Divine Source or First Cause of wealth, which is the Higher Power that is working in and through all of us. This Higher Power is labeled God, Spirit, Infinite, Divine, the Universe and is the eternal Source of everything that we will ever need or desire. Cash, stocks, bonds, savings, investments, real estate and employment are only external effects of tapping into the unlimited Source of supply within all of us. None of these material things would exist without the highest power in the universe providing and sustaining these things for us. Therefore, it is wise to get to the root of wealth – the thoughts, feelings and beliefs that create it. This book is all about repeatedly declaring your oneness with the abundance of the universe and manifesting a continuous uninterrupted flow of Money Blessings into your life.

Committing 40 consecutive days to the repetition of Money Blessings affirmations is about surrendering old habitual patterns and beliefs in order to create a new lifestyle. You will generate more satisfying results in your finances, relationships, and every area of your life when you keep your mind focused only on the prosperity you desire and the good that you want to manifest in your life experiences. During this process, when you are inspired or divinely guided towards some action, go for it!

After completing your first 40 consecutive days of *Money Blessings*, continue to repeat the affirmations over and over again in order to achieve even greater results. By using the Money Blessings affirmations in your daily life, you will constantly be attracting the prosperity you desire.

Most importantly, realize that as a Divine expression of God, you are here in this space and time to enjoy your life and unleash the unlimited potential within you. During your 40 days of Money Blessings, you will begin to notice expected and unexpected good showing up in your life in perfect and miraculous ways. Observe and be grateful for all of the signs that your new awareness of God as your supply is constantly increasing your prosperity.

Moreover, by purchasing this book, you have activated your faith in the all-sufficient supply of the universe. As you grow your wealth-consciousness, you will, of course, want to expose others to what is successfully working for you. Consider starting a Money Blessings Circle with colleagues, friends or family members and, together, commit to the Money Blessings affirmations for at least 40 consecutive days. Understand that there are others within your sphere of influence who also desire increased prosperity in their life experiences and you can help. Together, you all can share the unfolding of greater prosperity and enjoy more rewarding lives.

Right now, you have the opportunity to shift your focus to experiences of freedom and abundance by joining in a collective conscious of countless others who are also participating in the 40 Days of Money Blessings; thereby, making you a part of a powerful network of prosperous thinkers who are changing their lives for the better and the lives of others.

YOUR MONEY BLESSINGS EXPERIENCE

- For 40 consecutive days, read a Money Blessings affirmation aloud along with the supporting passage and scripture. A great time to do this is upon awakening in the morning to consciously set your intention on attracting Money Blessings throughout the day.

- After your daily reading, attempt to quiet yourself for a few minutes and think on the Money Blessings affirmation that you have just read. Notice any feeling of resistance to the new thought that you are dwelling upon. Past programming and conditioning may resurface as you are consistently adding new, healthier thoughts of abundance and prosperity to your mind.

- It is very helpful to write down thoughts and feelings each day as you work with the Money Blessings affirmations. Also, write down inspirations and ideas that come to you.

- You may be divinely led to take some type of action. If so, do not resist the guidance that you receive. Act upon it!

- Throughout the day, focus on and repeat, aloud or silently, your Money Blessings affirmation for the day. Be aware and grateful of new avenues of prosperity that open for you as a result of your new way of thinking.

- At night, before going to bed, it is helpful to reread your daily Money Blessings affirmation and its supporting passage and scripture. Give thanks for all evidence that new prosperity is blossoming in your life and will continue to manifest in your future as a reward for changing your thinking.

- HAPPY PROSPERING!

EVERY DAY
IS MY
PAY DAY!

Today's modern workforce has many people living from what they believe is one payday to the next. They learn to budget based on when they expect to get paid. Let's begin to shift our focus. Expect every day to be your payday. God's wealth is unlimited and ever present. You do not have to wait for it on a weekly or bi-weekly basis. See yourself as God's employee and expect to get paid by the universe on a daily basis.

AFFIRM: Every day is my pay day. I am one with the wealth of the universe and the wealth of the universe is one with me. Therefore, I expect to receive money and abundant resources on a daily basis. Each day, I prosper in multiple ways.

Give us this day our daily bread.
Matthew 6:11 (NASB)

I AM A
CHILD OF
ABUNDANCE.

You are a child of God. God is Abundance. Therefore, you are a child of abundance. There is no need to fear any kind of scarcity. Expect to always possess an abundance of good things. Expect to have an abundance of great relationships. Expect to have an abundance of money. Expect to have an abundance of energy and vitality. The universe will answer you according to your expectations and you will be richly rewarded.

AFFIRM: I am a child of abundance. I recognize God as the Source of all that is and all that ever will be. I acknowledge my oneness with the Creator of all. Therefore, I expect to always possess an abundance of good things. I expect to have an abundance of great relationships. I expect to have an abundance of money. I expect to have an abundance of energy and vitality. I am grateful to God for blessing me with the wonders that I am expecting.

You feed them from the abundance of your own house, letting them drink from your river of delights.
Psalm 36:8 (NLT)

MY TALENTS ARE ALWAYS PROFITABLE AND IN DEMAND.

There are talents that are very valuable within you. There is a treasure chest inside of you. These talents have been given to you to heal and bless the world. The world needs your talents and you will profit from sharing them with the world. The profits you generate from the proper use of your talents can bless many for generations to come.

AFFIRM: My talents are always profitable and in demand. I tap into the treasure chest within me and bring forth ideas that are very valuable. I heal and bless the world with my talents. As I uncover new talents, I utilize them to generate even more wealth. There is no limit to what I can do, have or be because I recognize the profitability of my talents.

A man's gift makes room for him and brings him before great men.
Proverbs 18:16 (NASB)

18

THE SOURCE
OF MY SUPPLY
IS ENDLESS!

God is the unlimited source of all supply. Know that, as a spiritual being, you can never run out of cash. Be grateful and enjoy all purchases, major and minor. Let go of any thoughts of lack and limitation. Instead, ask and allow Spirit to show you the way to an abundant life. There is no spot where God and money are not.

AFFIRM: The source of my supply is endless. I give my money and resources freely. My income can never be depleted because I know God is the only true source of all my supply. Therefore, I keep my money in circulation and send it forth to do good in the world. As a result, I see it return to me blessed and multiplied. I live in an unlimited universe and I claim my unlimited wealth now.

Wealth and riches are in his house,
and his righteousness endures forever.
Psalm 112:3 (NASB)

I SURVIVE
AND THRIVE!

God knows what you need. God also knows how all of your needs will be supplied. Unburden yourself from any stresses of financial obligations. Surrender all your cares to the ever-present Spirit of the Most High and know that you will never lack for any of life's necessities. See yourself as favored by the LORD, and richly prospering in every good way.

AFFIRM: I survive and thrive! All of my needs are divinely supplied. Therefore, I happily surrender all my cares to the ever-present Spirit of God knowing that I will never lack for any of life's necessities. God's good and perfect will for me is to prosper. I unburden myself from stresses of financial obligations. Instead, I see myself highly favored by the LORD and richly prospering in every way.

*Stay on the path that the LORD your
God has commanded you to follow.
Then you will live long and prosperous lives in the
land you are about to enter and occupy.
Deuteronomy 5:33 (NLT)*

BLESSINGS
FLOW TO ME
ABUNDANTLY
AND
FREQUENTLY
FROM EVERY
DIRECTION!

You do not have to wait for another lifetime to be blessed. Are you visualizing scarce blessings or abundant blessings? Call forth the Divine presence of abundance even in the midst of appearances. You can only achieve what your mind can conceive. Imagine abundant blessings flowing to you from expected and unexpected places.

AFFIRM: Blessings flow to me abundantly and frequently from every direction. I am open and receptive to Divine blessings. I deserve to be blessed. I am confident that I can achieve anything my mind can conceive. I see my blessings coming to me from all directions and I receive them with gratitude.

Your eyes will shine,
and your heart will thrill with joy,
for merchants from around the world will come to
you. They will bring you the wealth of many lands.
Isaiah 60:5 (NLT)

I AM THE RICHEST AND LUCKIEST PERSON I KNOW!

Oftentimes, we compare our luck or fortune to others. We may make statements like "He/She is so much richer or luckier than I," or "Knowing my luck …" followed by a negative statement. Did you know that you are the architect of your own luck? All good fortune is evidence of God's love and good will towards you. What you truly believe about yourself is what comes to pass. Why not consider yourself the richest and luckiest person you know?

AFFIRM: I am the richest and luckiest person I know. I enjoy all the good fortune that life has to offer. I expect to win often and to win big! I am grateful for God's love and good will towards me. I expect to be successful in all endeavors. Life feels good because I now create my own marvelous luck!

Beloved, I pray that in all respects you may prosper
and be in good health,
just as your soul prospers.
3 John 1:2 (NASB)

MY INCOME IS INCREASING.

Today is the day for you to accept your forthcoming financial blessings. See multiple channels of income flowing in your direction. Expect the promotion you have been dreaming about. See your business growing more and more profitable. Know that as your expectancy increases, Spirit will meet your demands with grace and ease.

AFFIRM: My income is increasing. I am grateful for multiple channels of income opening up for me right now. I increase my expectancy and Spirit meets my demands with grace, ease and in perfect ways.

You will enjoy the fruit of your labor.
How joyful and prosperous you will be!
Psalm 128:2 (NLT)

I BASK IN
UNLIMITED
SUCCESS!

Are you ready to live a successful life? Then, follow your dreams with confidence knowing that you are a child of God who has been designed to succeed. Celebrate the victories of successful living!

AFFIRM: I bask in unlimited success. I serve humanity with joy and celebrate the victories of successful living. I am a child of God; therefore, I follow my dreams with confidence because I have been designed to succeed.

Delight yourself in the LORD;
And He will give you the desires of your heart.
Psalm 37:4 (NASB)

I AM A
CREATIVE
MONEY MAKER!

You are one with God's infinite intelligence and overflowing abundance. Tap into the power within you that will enable you to create all the wealth you desire. Allow God to prosper you with all the ideas and resources you will ever need for every endeavor. Follow Divine guidance and watch money and resources miraculously appear in your life.

AFFIRM: I am a creative money maker. I tap into God's infinite intelligence and abundance to create wealth for myself and others. I believe I am a magnet for money attracting large sums regularly and easily. I follow Divine guidance and watch money and resources miraculously appear in my life to help me experience my hopes and dreams.

I walk in the way of righteousness,
in the midst of the paths of justice,
to endow those who love me with wealth,
that I may fill their treasuries.
Proverbs 8:20-21 (NASB)

I ENJOY
OPULENT
LIVING!

You need no special qualifications to receive the abundance of God. There is no need to struggle, beg or beseech God for the good that you deserve. Be open to your good just because you are who you are. You are good enough. You are worthy enough. Expect the Spirit of God to supply you with more than enough money to fulfill your heart's desire.

AFFIRM: I enjoy opulent living. I am worthy enough to receive God's best blessings. I thank God that I do not have to struggle or beg to receive my good. Instead, I am open and receptive to abundance flowing to me in larger and larger amounts. I expect rich rewards for being a child of God. Thank you, God, for lavish abundance in every area of my life.

May you be blessed by the LORD,
who made heaven and earth.
Psalm 115:15 (NLT)

I HAVE UNLIMITED ACCESS TO WEALTH.

You have unlimited access to God. All wealth comes from God. Therefore, you have unlimited access to the wealth of the universe. God exists through you and all life. Tap into the power within you and draw from Spirit that springs forth Infinite Abundance. There are no limits to the prosperity that you can enjoy.

AFFIRM: I have unlimited access to wealth. There are no limits to what I can do, have or be. Every area of my life is fantastic. I enjoy the fullness of the wealth upon the earth. I tap into the power within me and experience new abundance now and for evermore.

For "the earth is the LORD's, and everything in it."
1 Corinthians 10:26 (NLT)

I DESERVE THE BEST!

Your fondest wish is God's command! Create in your powerful mind an opulent lifestyle. God wants you to have the BEST of everything. The BEST health. The BEST finances. The BEST relationships. The BEST recreation. You deserve the BEST of everything. Only the BEST will do. Thank God for loving you so much that He lavishes you with nothing but the BEST.

AFFIRM: I deserve the BEST! I trust God to fulfill my fondest desires right here and now. I deserve the BEST of everything. I deserve the BEST just because I am me. I call forth my highest good and greatest joy from the Spirit within me.

Those who listen to instruction will prosper;
those who trust the LORD will be joyful.
Proverbs 16:20 (NLT)

I CAN AFFORD ALL THINGS THROUGH SPIRIT THAT PROSPERS ME.

There is no limitation or lack in the universe. God created mankind as the highest of life forms. Therefore we, as humanity, have dominion over all of the resources of the earth. It is all yours for being a joint heir to the kingdom of God. You can afford all that you desire. Just believe in the unfailing provision from the Source of all that is, was and will ever be.

AFFIRM: I can afford all things through Spirit that prospers me. I walk in authority expecting abundant increase in every area of my life. I know that as a joint heir to the kingdom of God, I am entitled to all that God is and has. I am grateful to know this Truth and I release all beliefs in limitation and lack. I put on the armor of prosperity and enlarge my vision for more.

I will give you the treasures of darkness
And hidden wealth of secret places,
So that you may know that it is I,
The LORD, the God of Israel,
who calls you by your name.
Isaiah 45:3 (NASB)

I SAVOR EACH AND EVERY MOMENT OF TODAY!

Savor today without conditions. All days are a blessing regardless of external conditions. God is sharing life more abundantly with you right now. Revel in it! The choices that you make today determine your experiences of tomorrow. Choose to be happy. Rejoice always and expect a life filled with wonderful memories!

AFFIRM: I savor each and every moment of today. I give praise and thanksgiving for all the possibilities that this day holds. I choose to be happy. My life is wonderful and is getting better and better with each passing day. My soul rejoices because today is a great day!

This is the day which the LORD has made;
Let us rejoice and be glad in it.
Psalm 118:24 (NASB)

PROSPEROUS LIVING IS FUN AND EASY!

Accept the abundance of God in every area of your life. Life is meant to be enjoyed to the fullest. Do not allow any obligations to destroy your belief that life is fun and easy. Instead, know that greater is God within you than any circumstances of the world.

AFFIRM: Prosperous living is fun and easy. I know that all of my obligations are divinely resolved. My mind is expanded beyond any negative beliefs and I expect prosperity now and always. Thank you God for a fun and prosperous life!

Take my yoke upon you.
Let me teach you,
because I am humble and gentle at heart,
and you will find rest for your souls.
For my yoke is easy to bear,
and the burden I give you is light.
Matthew 11:29-30 (NLT)

I ENJOY THE
FULLNESS OF
WEALTH!

Money is symbolic of wealth; however, real wealth is more than just money alone. Wealth is the ability to achieve optimum results in every area of your life. Good health is wealth. Having a sound mind is wealth. Great relationships are wealth. Lots of time to enjoy life is priceless. Real wealth, of course, also includes an abundance of financial resources as well.

AFFIRM: I enjoy the fullness of wealth. I do not limit wealth to finances. I know that I have more money than I will ever be able to spend. I choose to achieve optimum results in every area of my life. I enjoy a wealth of wonderful relationships. I am grateful for a sound mind and a loving heart. I have lots of time to enjoy my wealthy life. Life is good and I expect each day to get better.

And it is a good thing to receive wealth from God
and the good health to enjoy it.
To enjoy your work and accept your lot in life--
this is indeed a gift from God.
Ecclesiastes 5:19 (NLT)

MONEY GROWS
ON TREES.

Anyone who tells you that money does not grow on trees has no idea of how paper is made. The checks that you cash and spend were once part of a tree. The cash and checks that you circulate come from the vegetation you see every day. Look around at the lush greenery and know that you are looking at money in its purest form. God has given humanity the idea of how to convert wood and natural resources into spendable currency. The truth is money does grow on trees.

AFFIRM: Money grows on trees. The same God that supplies vegetation with water and sunshine provides me with what I need in order to grow more prosperous. As I see my pockets and wallet overflowing with cash, I am grateful to God for creating the vegetation of its origin. I know that all is good and God is the source of my supply.

And he shall be like a tree planted by the rivers of
water that brings forth his fruit in his season;
his leaf also shall not wither,
and whatsoever he does shall prosper.
Psalm 1:3

MY
MONEY WORKS
FOR ME!

You do not have to struggle to get more money because you do not have to struggle to get more God. Ask and you shall receive. Money is God in action. Allow God to be what you desire. Allow Spirit to work on your behalf by believing in its ever-present power.

AFFIRM: My money works for me. My money never runs out. I do not have to struggle to survive because God is working on my behalf. My money is working to bring me more money. I use the additional money to invest in more money-making opportunities.

Look at the birds.
They don't plant or harvest or store food in barns,
for your heavenly Father feeds them.
And aren't you far more valuable to him
than they are?
Matthew 6:26 (NLT)

I ALWAYS
HAVE A DIVINE
SURPLUS OF
GOOD THINGS.

You have chosen to think new thoughts about the source of your supply. The days of barely getting by are over! Spirit gives in abundance consistently and frequently. See yourself with more than enough money and resources to fulfill your heart's desires.

AFFIRM: I always have a Divine surplus of good things. I have overcome any belief in barely getting by. I have chosen to think new thoughts about the source of my supply. I know that Spirit gives to me abundantly with consistency and frequency. I see myself with more than enough money and resources to fulfill my heart's desires.

*But seek ye first the Kingdom of God
and His righteousness,
and all these things shall be added unto you.
Matthew 6:33*

I ATTRACT PROSPEROUS THINKERS.

Prosperous thinkers attract other prosperous thinkers. Like attracts like. Create a rich network of prosperous thinkers by keeping your mind focused on thoughts of prosperity. See the good in every situation and in every person. Behold the Spirit of God in all life and see life respond to you in glorious and remarkable ways.

AFFIRM: I attract prosperous thinkers. As I am, so shall I attract to me. I am a part of a rich network of prosperous thinkers. We keep our minds focused on wholeness, wealth, peace and joy. We behold the Spirit of God in all life. Our prosperous thinking transforms the circumstances of our community, nation and world for the better.

Both riches and honor come from You,
and You rule over all,
and in Your hand is power and might;
and it lies in Your hand to make great and to
strengthen everyone.
1 Chronicles 29:12 (NASB)

I ENJOY
SPENDING
MONEY ON
MYSELF AND
OTHERS.

Spending money on you is a wonderful habit. You deserve the best and are one with the inexhaustible source of supply. Spending money on others is a joy because it furnishes them with the desires of their hearts and makes them smile. As the master of your circumstances, spend lovingly and wisely on those you care about, especially yourself.

AFFIRM: I enjoy spending money on myself and others. I happily create a habit of giving to myself and others. I am one with the inexhaustible Source of all supply. I spend money lovingly and wisely to bring more joy into my life and the lives of others.

Give, and it will be given to you.
They will pour into your lap a good measure--
pressed down, shaken together, and running over.
For by your standard of measure
it will be measured to you in return.
Luke 6:38 (NASB)

MY WEALTH
BENEFITS THE
WORLD.

Your ability to create wealth for yourself provides you with the ability to create wealth for others. Your generous giving blesses others. Your successful business creates opportunities for many. You are able to afford you and your loved ones a lifestyle of luxury and comfort.

AFFIRM: My wealth benefits the world. I know that as I create wealth for myself, I create wealth for others too. My profitable business provides opportunities for many. I love my family and it is a pleasure to afford them a lifestyle of luxury and comfort. I bless others with my generous giving because I enjoy sharing my increased wealth with others.

To acquire wisdom is to love oneself;
people who cherish understanding will prosper.
Proverbs 19:8 (NLT)

GOD REVEALS WEALTH TO ME.

How much money do you desire to attract? Ask God, in earnest, to reveal to you the shortest, quickest and most harmonious way to generate the wealth you desire. Believe that you have already received it and give thanks.

AFFIRM: God reveals wealth to me. Each day, I ask the Spirit of God to direct me to my highest good and greatest joy. I trust the answers that are revealed to me and I believe that I already receive the good I desire. For this, I give thanks.

But you shall remember the LORD your God,
for it is He who is giving you power to make wealth,
that He may confirm His covenant which
He swore to your fathers, as it is this day.
Deuteronomy 8:18 (NASB)

MY
EARNINGS ARE
IMPRESSIVE!

You are rich! You've got it made! It is time to rejoice! Celebrate the Infinite Abundance flowing into your life now and always. No more scrimping and scraping just to get by. You feel inspired and bask in the glow of being a high earner!

AFFIRM: My earnings are impressive! I am rich! I've got it made! I celebrate the Infinite Abundance flowing into my life now and always. I rejoice in the glow of being a high earner. Life is great!

Give her the product of her hands,
And let her works praise her in the gates.
Proverbs 31:31 (NASB)

RICHES
ARE MY
BIRTHRIGHT.

You are the child of the King of kings. That makes you royalty by right of your birth. God's vast kingdom and everything in it belongs to you. The splendid things of life are yours for the asking. Focus your mind and heart on receiving your Divine inheritance. God loves you as His own and wants to bestow the bounty of the universe upon you.

AFFIRM: Riches are my birthright. I know that I am the child of the King of kings. I am royalty and I choose to live my life in the splendor of good things. My mind and heart are focused on receiving my Divine inheritance as a child of God. I am open to the bounty of the universe and receive good things.

Do not be afraid, little flock, for your Father has chosen gladly to give you the kingdom.
Luke 12:32 (NASB)

I ALWAYS
HAVE PLENTY
TO SHARE.

The wealth of the universe is unlimited. Tap into this power and you can generate countless blessings for yourself and others. There is always more than enough. When you share your good with others you open up for more good to flow into your life experiences.

AFFIRM: I always have plenty to share. I am one with the unlimited wealth of the universe. I tap into the power within me and generate blessings for myself and others. I am opening myself up to newer and greater experiences by constantly sharing my good with others.

And God will generously provide all you need.
Then you will always have everything you need and
plenty left over to share with others.
2 Corinthians 9:8 (NLT)

MY WILDEST DREAMS ARE POSSIBLE!

All things are possible to the person who believes. See your dreams manifesting in Divine time. You can be a best-selling author, a singer, a successful inventor or businessperson. The choice is yours. Dream Big! Act on your dreams as if they have already come true. The time and energy that you give to your dreams will richly reward you.

AFFIRM: My wildest dreams are possible. I know that all things are possible to the person who believes. Therefore, I see my dreams manifesting in Divine time. I choose to dream big. I confidently act on my dreams as if they have already become my reality. I am deeply grateful for a life of dreams fulfilled.

So I say to you, ask, and it will be given to you;
seek, and you will find;
knock, and it will be opened to you.
Luke 11:9 (NASB)

I RADIATE
AFFLUENCE.

In the spiritual realm, you are a field of radiating energy. The beliefs that you hold in your mind directly impact the energy you radiate. Picture yourself emitting an energy of affluence. People will respond to you differently as a result of your new way of thinking. You will become well-respected and well-loved. Others will know that good things happen when you are around.

AFFIRM: I radiate affluence. I know that the beliefs held in my mind are powerful and impact the energy that I radiate. I choose to emit the energy of prosperity. I am well-respected and well-loved. Others know that good things happen when I am around.

*Submit to God, and you will have peace;
then things will go well for you.*
Job 22:21 (NLT)

I ENJOY BOUNDLESS FINANCIAL SECURITY.

Banks keep money in safes. Many people store their valuables in safes. To them, safes represent security. However, the real security is in the Source of the riches. Hoarding money out of fear of loss stems from a belief in lack. There is no scarcity in the realm of Infinite Abundance. Anything that is yours by Divine right can never be taken away from you. Likewise, no good thing that God has for you can ever be withheld from you. Trust God as your financial security.

AFFIRM: I enjoy boundless financial security. I know that the real security lies in the Source of my wealth and not the money itself. I release all fears of losing riches. Instead, I acknowledge God as my financial security. All of my finances are safe because I trust the Divine power of protection.

Do not store up for yourselves treasures on earth,
where moth and rust destroy,
and where thieves break in and steal.
But store up for yourselves treasures in heaven,
where neither moth nor rust destroys,
and where thieves do not break in or steal.
Matthew 6: 19-20 (NASB)

I AM RICH AND POWERFUL BEYOND MEASURE.

There is no need to covet anyone's position or possessions. Your worth is priceless! If you choose to seek employment, do something you enjoy. Truthfully, you are always the boss of your own company. You have a choice of how you will spend your time, what services you will render and what activities you engage in to generate money.

AFFIRM: I am rich and powerful beyond measure. I am the boss of my own life and my own time. My worth is priceless. I commit my time to doing things I love. The work I do brings me wealth and fulfillment. No one is richer or more powerful than I, because I am one with the richest and most powerful force in the universe – God.

The blessing of the LORD makes a person rich,
and he adds no sorrow with it.
Proverbs 10:22 (NLT)

I AM A
BLESSED
GIVER!

People want to feel loved and appreciated. Gifts can warm hearts and bring smiles to the faces of others. Commit to being a generous giver. Birthdays, anniversaries and graduations are all opportunities to show your loved ones how special they are to you. However, sometimes the gifts that have the greatest impact are the ones that are given just because.

AFFIRM: I am a blessed giver. I recognize that my loved ones are a gift from God. Therefore, I make sure that I remind them of how special they are to me by blessing them with gifts given from the heart. I do not need a special occasion to give a gift. My giving to others makes me feel rich and happy.

The generous will prosper;
those who refresh others will themselves be refreshed.
Proverbs 11:25 (NLT)

SPIRIT
LEADS ME
TO THE BEST
INVESTMENTS.

The key to winning investments is right inside of you. Divine Wisdom knows exactly where you should put your money. Get still and ask Spirit to guide you in all of your investment decisions. Act on the guidance you are given and watch your wealth increase. God is the best financial advisor you can ever have.

AFFIRM: Spirit leads me to the best investments. I unlock the door of Divine Wisdom within me. I am certain that God knows exactly where I should invest my money. I trust the guidance of Spirit and profit greatly from wise investments.

Call to Me and I will answer you,
and I will tell you great and mighty things,
which you do not know.
Jeremiah 33:3 (NASB)

MY LIFE IS A HEAVENLY EXPERIENCE.

Use your power of imagination to create mental molds for God's Infinite Abundance to fill. It is up to you what you will create. Dare to create your heart's desires. See the very best things happening to you, for you and around you. Each day, expect to experience heaven on earth.

AFFIRM: My life is a heavenly experience. I imagine my world filled with peace, good health, fantastic relationships, great finances and free time to do things that I enjoy. God's Infinite Abundance responds by giving me exactly what I desire. The very best things are happening to me now and always.

I will give you the keys of the kingdom of heaven;
and whatever you bind on earth shall have been
bound in heaven, and whatever you loose on earth
shall have been loosed in heaven.
Matthew 16:19 (NASB)

I AM RICH TODAY AND WILL BE EVEN RICHER TOMORROW.

Right where you are today, you have the wealth of the universe at your disposal. Everything in the visible world manifests from an invisible Source. Therefore, there is no reason to believe that there can be an absence of any good thing from your life experiences. The Truth is that there is abundance all around you waiting for you to open your heart and mind to accept your share.

AFFIRM: I am rich today and will be even richer tomorrow. As I grow my wealth consciousness, money and resources rapidly increase to reward my new way of thinking. I have the wealth of the universe at my disposal right here and now. I open my heart to accept my share of the Infinite Abundance that is enfolding me now.

I have riches and honor,
as well as enduring wealth and justice.
Proverbs 8:18 (NLT)

I ENJOY LIFE
TO THE
FULLEST!

Dare to be a winner at the game of life. Life is meant to be enjoyed. Today is your opportunity to throw off any mental shackles of doubt and fear. Declare God's blessings and supernatural favor over every area of your life. Walk boldly under the banner of victory!

AFFIRM: I enjoy life to the fullest. I choose to win at the game of life. Old thoughts of doubt and fear are history. I declare God's blessings and supernatural favor over every area of my life. Today, I walk confidently under the banner of victory! Savoring each wonderful moment, I thank God for a life of wealth and fulfillment.

They will live in prosperity,
and their children will inherit the land.
Psalm 25:13 (NLT)

MY EARNINGS GREATLY EXCEED MY EXPENSES.

Your life is a reflection of your habitual thinking. Everything that you are experiencing now first began as a thought in your mind. Debt happens when your expenses exceed your earnings. What you earn today is your choice. You agreed to work for the salary you are receiving now. Therefore, if you desire to increase your earnings, think new thoughts and make new choices. You are worth it!

AFFIRM: My earnings greatly exceed my expenses. Past choices have no power over my future earnings. I choose to see an abundant financial surplus after I have paid all of my bills. I use the extra cash to reward myself for thinking better thoughts and making healthier choices. Greater is the wealth that is within me than the financial obligations of the world.

The LORD will open for you His good storehouse, the heavens, to give rain to your land in its season and to bless all the work of your hand; and you shall lend to many nations, but you shall not borrow.
Deuteronomy 28:12 (NASB)

I FOCUS ONLY ON PROSPERITY.

Your mind is your most valuable possession. Every day, people vie for your attention in an attempt to influence your thinking. Choose to focus only on prosperity. Have the courage to block out harmful distractions. You are the master of your mind. As a result, you become the master of your experiences. Direct your thoughts and actions only on the wonderful results you desire to achieve.

AFFIRM: I focus only on prosperity. I recognize the importance of keeping my thoughts centered on Infinite Abundance. I see the good in every thing and every one. I block out any thoughts or suggestions that do not serve my highest good and greatest joy. I expect that the prosperity that I focus on will manifest in my life, world and affairs.

Meditate upon these things;
give thyself wholly to them;
that thy profiting may appear to all.
1 Timothy 4:15 (KJV)

MY PROSPERITY PRAYERS ARE ANSWERED QUICKLY WITH GRACE AND EASE.

God loves you just as you are. Begin each new day with a fresh awareness that your path to unlimited wealth is guided by Spirit. Give thanks for answered prayers knowing that everything works on your behalf.

AFFIRM: My prosperity prayers are answered quickly with grace and ease. Situations that once looked bleak have been transformed into sown seeds of blessings. I rejoice in my new awareness that my road to unlimited wealth is guided by Spirit. I happily give thanks for answered prayers believing that all things work on my behalf.

Therefore I say to you,
all things for which you pray and ask,
believe that you have received them,
and they will be granted you.
Mark 11:24 (NASB)

I AM EMPOWERING MYSELF AND OTHERS TO GREATER PROSPERITY.

The mind, once expanded to accept higher and greater thoughts, can never shrink back to its old dimensions. You have chosen to create a new life of prosperity by committing to growing your Spirit of wealth. Continue to feed your consciousness with thoughts of abundance. Tune into the voice of God within you for direction. Know that it is a new day that you have chosen to experience in a wealthier, new way.

AFFIRM: I am empowering myself and others to greater prosperity. I have expanded my awareness to the point of accepting unlimited wealth as my very own. I happily grow richer and richer because of my new way of thinking. I know that my mind, once enlarged to greater dimensions, can never return to old limited beliefs. It is a new day and I expect to experience life in a wealthier new way!

"For I know the plans I have for you," says the LORD.
"They are plans for good and not for disaster,
to give you a future and a hope."
Jeremiah 29:11 (NLT)

NOTES

NOTES

NOTES

_____

_____

_____

_____

_____

_____

_____

_____

_____

_____

_____

_____

NOTES

_____

_____

_____

_____

_____

_____

_____

_____

_____

_____

_____

_____

NOTES

_____

_____

_____

_____

_____

_____

_____

_____

_____

_____

_____

_____

NOTES

_____

_____

_____

_____

_____

_____

_____

_____

_____

_____

_____

NOTES

NOTES

NOTES

NOTES

_____

_____

_____

_____

_____

_____

_____

_____

_____

_____

_____

_____

ORDER FORM

Mail with check/money order enclosed or credit card information to:

Fax to: 1-888-208-4317

Empower House Publishing, LLC
222 Broadway, 19th Floor
New York, NY 10038

Qty	Title	Price	
	Money Blessings	$12.99 x PER BOOK	
	U.S. Shipping	$3.99 x PER BOOK	
		Total	

Order online now at www.moneyblessings.com. **PayPal**™

❏ Check /Money Order   ❏ Visa   ❏ MasterCard   ❏ American Express

_____   _____
Card Number   Security Code (CVV2, CVC2, CID)

_____   _____
Expiration Date   Signature

Ship to: _____
_____
_____
_____

Money Blessings is available at special quantity discounts for bulk purchase for sales promotions, fundraising and educational needs. Special books or book excerpts also can be created to fit specific needs. For details, write Empower House Publishing, Special Markets, 222 Broadway, 19th Floor, New York, NY 10038 or email at orders@moneyblessings.com.

Money Blessings

Book Design by Kanika McKerson and Lakia Ross
Editing by Marilyn Coates and Kelley Bass Jackson

Made in the USA
Middletown, DE
14 September 2020